LOVELY LUTRADUR

MARION BARNETT AND DIJANNE CEVAAL

LOVELY LUTRADUR
Marion Barnett and Dijanne Cevaal
© M Barnett, D Cevaal 2008
('Lutradur' used by kind permission of Freudenberg.)

Published by Artmixter
ISBN No 978-0-9563006-0-7

Acknowledgements:
We would like to thank Mervyn Williams and the staff of Spunart for their unfailing courtesy and assistance.

Printed in Great Britain by the MPG Books Group, Bodmin and King's Lynn

Lovely Lutradur

Contents

Lovely Lutradur

Introduction

Every textile artist has a dream material. When we compared notes, we found that we both wanted something similar, despite our differences in approach to art. Dijanne's work is based on nature, Marion, on the other hand, works mainly in abstract. We both have very different cultural backgrounds, too. Dijanne is based in Australia, but was born in the Netherlands, Marion in England, but was born in Scotland. But our work does have some things in common; both of us use strong colours and are fascinated by texture and layer.

So, what was it we had in common when it came to cloth? This dream material should be as easy to work with as cotton, as transparent as silk organza, and have sheen like silk. Oh, and it shouldn't fray, and should tolerate high temperatures. After a bit of searching, we have finally found our dream material; its name is Lutradur.

So, why Lutradur? Well, for Marion, it is the see through nature of the cloth. The fibres are floated across each other in the manufacturing process, producing a material which is similar in texture to fibreglass, but without the problems of shedding, etc, that fibreglass has. Even the heaviest weight of Lutradur has this see through nature, and it produces wonderful layered effects in work, that could previously only be obtained by working with silk sheers, which are expensive and difficult to work with.

For Dijanne the lure of Lutradur is the ability to colour with brilliant light fast colour and to control the application of colour. Transparency and layering are also important factors as is the materials ability to "breathe" like natural materials. It has a seductive sheen and the texture when worked upon visually appears like felt, thereby adding richness. The material is remarkably sturdy and stable for sewing as Dijanne sews her work very intensively both by machine and hand. The materials tolerance to high temperatures makes it ideal for such things as foiling and controlled melting. However it is the intensity of colour and the play of colour achieved with layering that appeals to Dijanne's sense of colour and contrast.

For both of us, though, it adds a dimension to our work that we truly enjoy. We hope you will, too. And we hope this book will inspire you to work with this wonderful material!

Using This Book

This book is split into three sections. In the first, you will find an overview of Lutradur, and how to colour it. In the second, there are a series of projects which we undertook to demonstrate how versatile Lutradur is. Each has an explanation of what we did, and how to do that yourself using your own ideas. The third and final section is a gallery of work, with a few notes as to what techniques were used to make each piece. You can read the book from cover to cover, or dip into whatever section seems most interesting to you at the time. Looking for something in particular? Remember you can use the 'edit, find' function in your browser to find key words in the text.

 This book is a learning tool; use it however suits you best! To make the most of it, though, you might wish to work with a journal, keeping notes of what you do, and how you did it. It is always useful for future reference. You could even make the cover from Lutradur, as Dijanne has here!

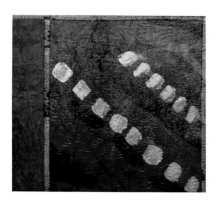

Section One : Learning About Lutradur

What IS Lutradur?

Lutradur is a non woven polyester fabric intended for industrial uses, which range from the purely decorative through to the fiercely practical. Lutradur is the trade name of Freudenberg, who produce a wide range of non woven fabrics, both for industry and the home dressmaking market (most textile artists use Vilene, for example, another of their product ranges), though the name has come to be used as a generic for cloth of this type. Like all kinds of material, Lutradur comes in a variety of different weights, and you should experiment with them to see which you prefer. The Lutradur made by Freudenberg is currently available to artists in 30gm, 70gm,100gm and 130gm weights; the lower the number, the lighter, and therefore more transparent the cloth. There are other cloths made in a similar way to Lutradur. Known as 'fine denier spunbonded polyesters', they are lighter in weight than Lutradur, and come in a variety of colours, all of which can be overdyed and coloured just like Lutradur. There are also cloths sold as 'florist wrapping' which are highly textured, and may similarly be used in the same way as Lutradur. However, not all of these are heat resistant; be sure to try it out before you invest in it!

Even the heaviest weight of Lutradur retains some transparency, but in general, we have found the following.

- **30gm**, the lightest of the four, is ideal for transparent effects. Use it over all kinds of different cloth, patterned or plain (this is also true for the non industrial versions of Lutradur).
- **70gm** has fair transparency, but is better used with patterned fabric if you wish to gain the full benefit of the transparency effect.
- **100** and **130**gm are the heaviest of the four, and can be run through a computer printer as if they were paper. However, they do need to have a very strongly contrasting patterned fabric beneath them for the transparency effect to be really clear, preferably black and white,

though other strong contrasts between light and dark also work, it is worth experimenting with this. Both are suitable for 3D applications, such as bookmaking. They are also ideal for making banners, or embroidered wall hangings.

All four weights of Lutradur can be coloured in exactly the same way, using transfer dyes, paints, pencils, crayons etc, as is described throughout the pages of this book. It is also possible to fuse two layers together, with the thinner layer on top, making a stable, easy to use cloth just ready to stitch.

You can see how much the transparency decreases in the following sequence of images. In each case, a piece of plain white Lutradur, one of each weight, has been placed on top of a black and white lino printed paper with a little bit of added watercolours. As you can see, the first image comes through very clearly, but as the Lutradur gets heavier, the image gets less distinct. You really do need to take this into consideration when you are choosing which weight of Lutradur to use in a particular project. There is nothing more frustrating than having the right piece of coloured Lutradur in the wrong weight for your project!

30 Gm Lutradur. You can see it is very transparent and that the underlying fabric with motif can be seen quite clearly. This of course gives you lines for stitching, further mark making or cutting or melting away.

70 gm Lutradur. Here, the fibres are much more densely packed, yet it is still possible to discern the underlying motif. The colours are much less noticeable, but it would still be easy to follow the lines of the bold motif.

100gm Lutradur (right), and much less of the image is coming through. Where the underlying fabric is strongly contrasted in colours, it is still possible to see most of the motif, and there is much less colour visible. 130gm (below) produces a similar result.

But Polyester… Won't It Melt?

Polyester cloth gets a bad name in quilting circles, for any number of reasons. Recently, though, textile artists have been using polyesters, plastics and all kinds of man made materials to good effect, usually by colouring and melting them. And yes, you are right, Lutradur *will* melt if you apply a soldering iron or heat gun. The heat of an ordinary iron, however, will not melt it unless you choose to, by extending the amount of time you have the iron in contact with the cloth. Some of the effects we show you in this book are produced by distressing Lutradur using heat; most of them, however, rely on the domestic iron transferring colour to the cloth.

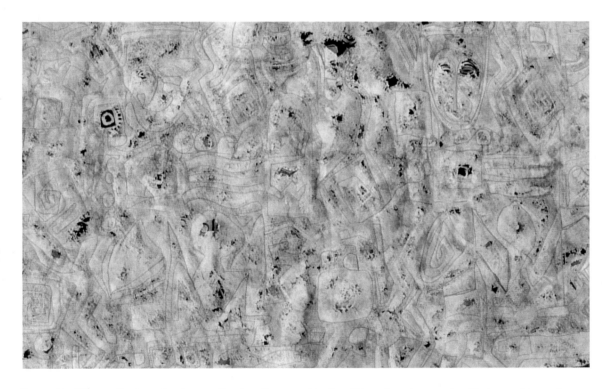

Lost In Translation features Lutradur melted with a heat gun to distress it and show elements of the cloth beneath it.

Adding Colour To Lutradur

Lutradur can be coloured in the same way as any other polyester fabric, using transfer dyes, acrylic paint, silk or fabric paint, pens, pencils etc. Just follow the instructions for each product that are provided by the manufacturer. We both use transfer dye extensively with Lutradur, as it results in strong vibrant colours, and is the most flexible of media to use with this extremely flexible cloth.

Transfer dye can be bought in a number of forms; as a powder, as premixed colour ready to paint or in liquid form which requires the addition of water. It is also available in crayon form, which is useful for making delicate marks, line drawings etc, but is less useful for backgrounds. All lead to similar results with brilliant colour. However, if you intend to colour large areas of cloth, you might wish to avoid the premixed ready to use colours, as they come in small amounts. We have found buying the transfer dye in powder form to be the most economical. Crayons, too, are very inexpensive, and are useful to have in your armoury of methods for colouring Lutradur; a selection is shown below. Note the jam jar; this contains transfer die solution.

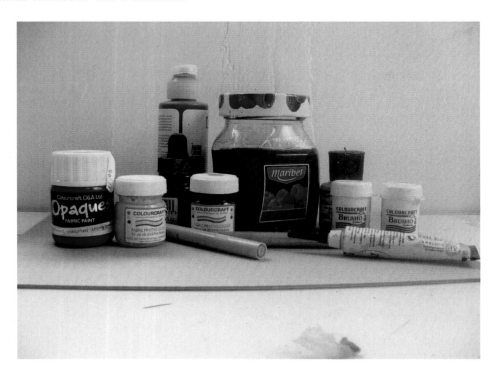

RECIPE/METHOD FOR MIXING TRANSFER DYE FROM POWDER

Mix the dye powder into a paste with just enough boiling water to dissolve it (see health and safety guidance above), and then add cold water to the required strength. There are no set rules as to how much water should be used; however, as a guide, 10g per 100 ml will give full intensity and 3g per 100 ml will produce pastel shades. (1 teaspoon of dye weighs approximately 5 grams).

If you are using the transfer dye solution follow the manufacturer's instructions for the quantity of water that will need to be added. Once it is mixed up, it is used in the same way as the mixed transfer dye powder.

It is possible to buy a range of transfer dye powders. However, a wide palette of colours can be mixed from a combination of Canary Yellow (or Lemon Yellow) Golden Yellow, Magenta (or Red), Turquoise, Mid Blue and Black. When mixing, remember that the colour that you paint on the paper will not be the same as the colour which appears once the transfer process has been completed. The same principles apply to premixed transfer dyes. If you wish to print, paint or screenprint, transfer dyes can be thickened with DR-33 paste, known as Indalca in the UK (check with the dye supplier as names for this thickener differ from country to country). Manutex, the thickener used for Procion MX, is not suitable for use with transfer dyes. Thickened dye produces sharper clear lines. It must be remembered that every nuance of texture, however insignificant, will be faithfully reproduced during heat transfer.

Once mixed, the colours can be applied to the paper in layers so that in the transfer process those colours applied first will show up in the second or third print. This produces interesting and random variations in each transfer print, making each unique.

Storage

Once the powders have been made into solution with water, it is possible to store the dyes in a container which can be closed, indefinitely. Should the powders dry out, however, it is possible to add more water to them and they can be used again. It is a good idea to keep them in a cool place.

Painting The Papers

The next stage of the process consists of painting the design onto paper by any method, such as printing, mark making with crayons, painting, rolling the paint. After the paper has dried, the design is placed face down onto the fabric and then subjected to heat and pressure. The heat transfers the dye on the paper to the Lutradur creating a permanent bond .The final result is brilliant colour which is fast to light and washing.

Almost any paper can be used for your design; though best results are obtained by using thin, non absorbent paper with a shiny surface eg. Litho paper. We have found that normal photocopy paper works well, as does newsprint. When the colours on the paper dry, they may appear dull and uninteresting. Don't panic! The colour on the fabric will be much brighter, and a few surprises will appear especially if you have mixed the colours yourself.

Brush strokes do not transfer to the Lutradur if the paper is painted evenly. You can paint the papers in any direction at all, as it does not make any significant difference to the transfer process. However you can be very intentional in creating brush strokes (dry brushing) in which case they will transfer. Where you see a defined mark on the paper, you will see that same mark on the cloth.

It is possible to paint your papers beforehand and store them for when you are ready. This is a good thing to do on a hot summer day in the garden; just make sure that it isn't too windy! It's a fun thing to do with friends; Marion has dye painting parties in her garden every so often.

Your papers must be dry before you stack them. If you are in a hurry, you can dry them with a hair dryer.

The hand painted papers that are produced by this process can be beautiful in their own right, and may be used for collage once exhausted.

Cleaning Up

It is easy to clean up after using transfer paints. Simply wash your brushes, lino-cuts and stamps under warm running water and scrub with a brush to clean. Dijanne lives with a septic tank system, so she cleans up in a bucket.

Health And Safety

For Health and Safety reasons make sure that you are working in a well ventilated area when working with the iron/press. If you have lung problems, e.g. asthma, you should wear a respirator; consult your doctor if you have concerns. Set your iron to NO STEAM. The interaction of the steam against the paper can send a nasty spray of hot steam towards the hand holding the iron.

Transferring Colour To Fabric

The success of transferring the design onto fabric will depend largely on the type and temperature of heating equipment used. Best results will be achieved with a transfer press, but a laundry press or similar may also be used. When using a press, however, it is essential to experiment with the Lutradur and transfer papers, to see how long to leave them in the press; if you leave the Lutradur too long in the press, it will melt. Marion has a press, and finds that times can vary, but that she needs about six to eight seconds on a fully heated press at maximum heat to produce the transfer effect. This will vary from press to press, so be sure to check. You may find that the lighter grades of Lutradur will melt more quickly, particularly those sold as decorative florist paper.

It really isn't necessary to rush out and buy a press, however. An iron is just as effective, if a little slower, and gives you much more control over the end result. If your iron has steam holes move the iron around, being careful not to leave hole marks on the cloth. An iron shaped darker patch may be attractive, but only if you really want it there as part of the design! This is also a consideration when using a laundry press, by the way, which is, after all, shaped like a large iron. Marion transfers her larger sheets of paper using an iron for that very reason.

The Transfer Process

Make sure that your painted papers are completely dry before you begin the transfer process. Any wetness will cause the paper to adhere to the polyester fibres, and is then difficult to remove.

To transfer your design it is best to place a sheet of paper or pelmet Vilene on your ironing board or press base. Place the Lutradur on top of this and then place your painted design face down onto the Lutradur. It is a good idea to tape the design onto the Lutradur to prevent it moving. When using a press, add another piece of paper on top of the paper/cloth sandwich (this stops the dye transferring to the cloth on the top side of the press). Then, when your iron has been heated to its hottest setting, press down for a period of time, say, 10- 20 seconds, and then carefully move it. You can check whether the transfer is taking place by carefully lifting a corner of the transfer sheet. It is possible to get 3 prints from one piece of painted paper, although the intensity of colour will reduce with each transfer. It is *essential* that your iron be very hot when you begin the process. And remember, no steam!

Overview : The Process In Pictures

Follow Dijanne, as she takes you through the process of making a piece of work from start to finish.

Painting the Papers

As you know, the process starts with painting the papers, in this instance with purchased premixed transfer dyes. The process is exactly the same with dyes you have mixed yourself. If you do not want the colours to run into each other, we suggest it is best to paint the background on a separate sheet, and the detail, in this case the dark shape, on a separate sheet of paper. This paper has several layers and I waited for each stage to dry before I painted the next layer. Layering the colours in this way can cause interesting effects in the second and third prints as the colours that were applied first tend to come through in later prints.

If you want to have a clean edge to your painted papers, make sure you continue the paint right to the edge of the paper. If there is no colour on the paper, no matter how small a speck, it will be left as white when you transfer the image to the Lutradur. If this does happen, however, simply mask off the edge of the image on the cloth, move your painted paper so that it covers the missing part of the image, and iron again.

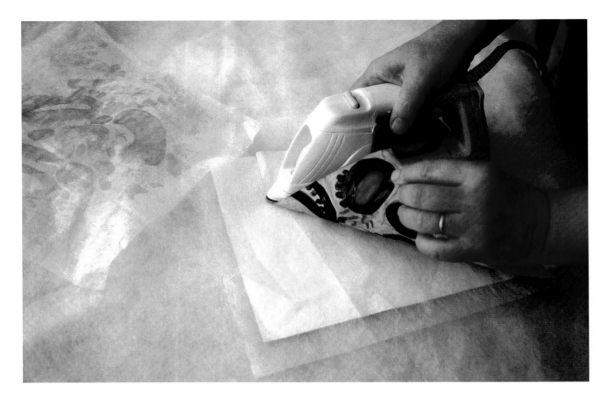

Transferring the painted paper onto the Lutradur

When transferring the image from painted paper onto the Lutradur, it is important to keep your iron in the same place for at *least* 5 seconds otherwise the colour will not transfer in its full strength. If using a steam iron, the holes of the steam iron will also play a role in the transfer process, so it *is* important to move the iron. It is possible to print the same piece of paper two to three times which is of course wonderful if you want to create a related series of work, though you should bear in mind that each print will be fainter than the one before.

Once this stage is completed, the Lutradur is ready to use.

Layering the backing, wadding, underlying fabric and Lutradur

Once the dye has been transferred from paper to cloth, the colour is permanent and you are now ready for the next step, which is layering the material. In this instance, Dijanne is making a quilted piece, and so has used a backing fabric, wadding, another fabric under the Lutradur and then the Lutradur itself. The whole is pinned together ready for sewing. The colour of the fabric placed underneath the Lutradur plays an important role in the final appearance of the Lutradur, particularly if the Lutradur is lightweight and very transparent. This effect is diminished the heavier (and therefore less transparent) the weight of the Lutradur.

And voila! The images below show detail of the finished stitched pieces, in this case, elements of a large piece, 'It Is A Hot Continent'. These images clearly show how the colour of the fabric underneath the Lutradur plays an important role in establishing the colour of the finished piece. They also show how the colour of thread can add to the visual impact of the finished piece. Each piece of transfer printed Lutradur in 'It Is A Hot Continent' was the same colour. The careful choice of a variety of different colours underneath it has very clearly affected the final outcomes, whilst the thread also adds an element of contrast.

Detail from "It's a Hot Continent": Lutradur with red fabric underneath and blue stitching

Detail from "It's a Hot Continent": Lutradur with blue fabric underneath and red and turquoise stitching

Detail from" It's a Hot Continent": Lutradur with yellow fabric underneath and blue and red stitching

"It's a Hot Continent"

And finally, the finished piece. Remember, the top layer of Lutradur in *all* of these small pieces was the same colour. This piece was inspired by the topography of Australia. Dijanne frequently flies to other parts of the world and on the return journey, she flies over the vast continent where she lives. The river shape and water hole shapes are interesting and the colouring often spectacular.

These projects are meant to inspire you, but also to show you how differently we work with the same materials. Just as everyone's work is different, each person's process is uniquely their own. There are no rights and wrongs to this; just personal preference. We hope that you will pick out the elements from each of our personal practices that suit the way you work, and integrate them.

Project 1 : Cutting Away/Reverse Applique

Lutradur is extremely stable to work with and as a result it can be cut away very easily once sewn or indeed melted with a soldering iron. I prefer to cut it away as it is possible to burn the underlying fabric if your soldering iron is too hot. Another effect of using the soldering iron is that it can create a hard edge where the fibre has melted because it is after all a polyester fibre. This may of course be just the effect you are after! Lutradur cuts away very easily and leaves a clean edge that does not fray where it has been cut. I tend to cut away the Lutradur after the quilting process, as this anchors the Lutradur in place, ready for cutting.

I usually layer my fabrics ready for quilting and stitching at the same time. I therefore have a backing fabric, batting, fabric and Lutradur which I have coloured and perhaps printed. I pin this sandwich at regular intervals and commence stitching around the motifs where I want to reveal the background fabric. This helps secure the Lutradur as well. Once the stitching is in place, you can trim away the Lutradur with good sharp scissors or with your soldering iron. In essence this technique is one of reverse appliqué.

In the first example shown here, I have hand painted the background fabric, layered the Lutradur on top. The areas inside the orange stitched areas have been cut away to reveal the underlying hand painted fabric. Likewise the snake like squiggles have been cut away to reveal the underlying colour. Stitching has been used to accentuate the outlines of the revealed cut away areas. Lutradur's pleasing transparency allows the motifs of the underlying fabric to be visible and provide clues for stitching . I also like to use contrasting coloured threads to add visual interest and line. For me stitching is definitely a mark making tool!

The images below, elements from four different pieces of work, illustrate the process beautifully. You can see the difference in both colour and texture between the Lutradur areas and the cut away areas, where the underlying cotton fabric is exposed. Cutting away can expose texture, pattern, shape and colour, whichever you choose to highlight.

A detail from "Rock Pools (above)

"Inspired By Paisley" (left)

This small stitched piece had the Lutradur placed onto a yellow background fabric, which was stitched and the sections which are now yellow were carefully cut away. The Lutradur in this piece was not as transparent as in the Rockpools piece, so cutting away has been used to create contrast and texture. The colour of the thread was again an important consideration.

"X Marks the Place" (right)

The crosses were first sewn by machine and then carefully cut away, exposing the underlying blue fabric. It has then been hand stitched with hand dyed crochet cotton. Lutradur is extremely amenable to hand stitching and the lighter the weight of the Lutradur the more easily it is stitched. The hand stitching creates an interesting crinkle in the texture, particularly when using the light weight lutradur.

Dreamaway Tree (above) has had the tree motif painted onto papers and then transferred to the Lutradur. It has been stitched with Valdani cotton variegated thread in 35 weight weight, which has created a pleasing texture. In the upper part of the tree, there are dark "spots". These have been created by melting away some of the Lutradur by lightly touching the spots with a soldering iron.

Project Two : Printing

It is extremely easy to print with transfer dyes/paints. I like to work with lino-cuts which I have carved myself, but this technique will work successfully with commercially made plates, blocks, rubber stamps etc. One simply paints the transfer paint (the paints that are in solution) onto the lino cut with a brush, making sure the paint is spread evenly. The painted lino cut is then placed face down onto the paper and pressed in order to transfer the print. I find that I need to work very quickly using this method in our hot Australian summers as the paint dries very quickly. If the image smudges or blobs a little it means that too much transfer paint has been painted onto the lino cut, or it is too wet. If the image is patchy then too little paint has been applied. It is a matter of experimenting and finding which consistency is right for you- you may intend to have smudged or patchy effects in a particular piece.

When printing, it is important to find a surface with enough give to take the imprint cleanly yet with enough firmness to make it sharp and clean. If your image is blotchy, it is often the result of your printing mat being too hard. Similarly, if the image is fuzzy, it is often the result of your printing mat being too soft. I use carpet underlay covered with clear plastic table cloth material and find this works well.

Anything that has a relief surface can be used for printing- e.g. ivy leaves, wattle tree leaves, geranium leaves, herringbone ferns, bracken leaves, maple leaves, potato mashers, bubble wrap plastic, lino cuts, stamps, orange bags, anything you choose or have to hand!

The first example is using a relief print to create the print, in this case a small Ethiopian stone bible (below right).

Detail of Stone Angels- finished piece

The paint was painted onto the carved stone image and then "stamped"onto the paper.

Printing With Lemon Halves

In this instance a lemon was cut in half and the transfer dye painted onto the cut lemon. The lemon was quite wet, so I put the slightly thickened transfer paint onto a foam rubber printing pad and pressed the lemon into that, and this was then pressed onto the paper, but not too hard as the lemon has quite a lot of juice. All kinds of fruit and vegetables can be used in this way; remember making potato cuts as a child?

This piece was both hand stitched and machine stitched for definition and greater texture. The turquoise coloured shapes were cut away to create contrast and visual impact. See a larger, detail image on the following page.

Detail, Lemon Study

Printing with Lino Cuts.

Preparing the papers for transfer printing (above)

Painting the transfer paint onto the linocut with a brush. Make sure you spread the paint as evenly as possible (although interesting effects can be obtained with partial coverage as well.

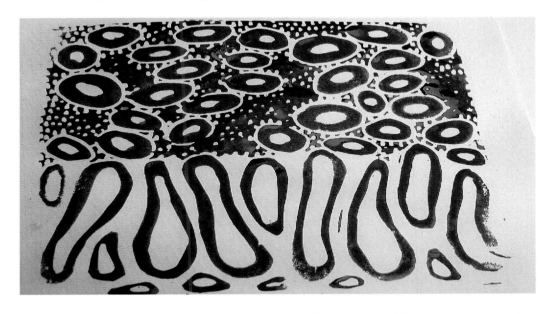

(above) The lino cut printed onto the transfer paper (this is just normal photocopying paper)

Transferring the linocut print onto the coloured Lutradur (above).

The linocut has been transferred and layered and stitched (above). Contrasting threads have been used to create interest as well as a hand printed background fabric. This piece was inspired by a tiny fragment of coral I found on a Queensland beach some years ago (below).

Project 3 : Foiling

Foiling can be done in two ways. Firstly it can be done with fusible web, ie vliesofix/bondaweb/wondaweb, in which case the desired shape is cut out from the fusible web and ironed onto the Lutradur. The foil is laid over the top, foil side up. One then places a Teflon ironing mat or a piece of greaseproof paper over the whole and then press firmly with an iron. You do have to wait for the foil to cool down before peeling it off, otherwise the foil will not adhere properly to the fusible web. Once the foil has cooled down, the foil paper can be removed and you are left with the foil attached to the Lutradur.

This motif (left) has been inspired by the Roman carvings at Palmyra in Syria which was once one of the great cities on the silk road. The motif has been drawn onto the fusible webbing on the paper side.

The next step in the process is to iron the fusible webbing, paper side up, onto the Lutradur.

Peeling the paper off to reveal the fusible web adhering to the Lutradur.

The foil is then laid over the area where the fusible webbing is adhered, with the foil side facing up (above). You then lay a Teflon mat or thick Vilene over the foil and iron, with the iron set on dry for several minutes. Allow the foil to cool completely and then peel off (below).

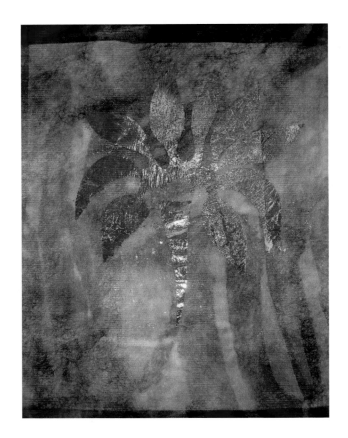

The motif foiled onto the Lutradur is now ready for further work (above). You need to be careful in handling the foiled piece as the fusible webbing/foil combination is a bit brittle and it can flake off if handled too much.

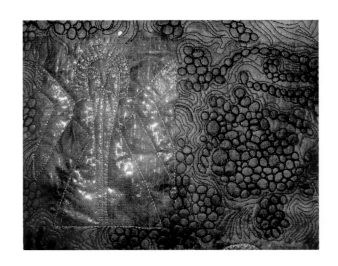

Detail of Stone Angels IV (right)

Stone Angels IV (left)

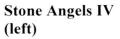

The second method for foiling is using a specialised glue (available from various suppliers listed in the back of the book). The glue is applied with a paint brush, and must be left at least 24 hours to be dry. If you are in a desperate hurry, you can dry the glue with a hair dryer, but you do have to make sure the glue is well and truly dry before applying the foil. If the glue is wet, the foil will not attach to the glue. Once the glue is dry, you lay the foil paper over the glue, foil side up, place a Teflon mat over the whole and iron. Again you must wait for the foil to cool completely for best results. When cool, peel off the foil.

Hand painting the foiling glue onto pre-printed Lutradur leaves (above)

"Gum Leaves" (above)

A stencil has been created with heavy weight Vilene, again using the Palmyra palm motif.

Applying the textile glue to the Lutradur. Be careful not to create big blobs of glue, as they take much longer to dry.

The foil is laid over the dried glue in exactly the same manner as with the fusible webbing. Because the glue was not spread thickly, the foil only adheres to areas with glue, giving a rather pleasing worn effect. The glue foil bond is much more stable than the fusible web foil bond.

The images above show the comparison of a foiled piece with fusible webbing (left) and a foiled piece with textile glue.

Project Four : Lutradur Postcards

The fashion for fabric postcards is continuing unabated. I enjoy working at that size (4" by 6"), but prefer the double size (8" by 6"), and rather than sending them, I like to give them as gifts, ready to mount and frame. And after swearing that I would never work that small, I recently began to make ACEOs (Artists Cards Editions and Originals), which you may know as ATCs, or Artists Trading Cards. (The difference is simple; you can sell an ACEO, but you always trade ATCs). These are 2.5" by 3.5" in size. The image below shows templates for all three sizes.

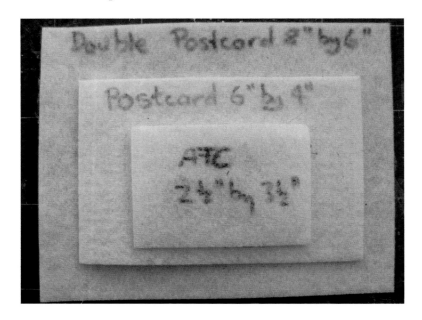

I recently made a series of small lino prints intended for a double sized postcard, using printing inks intended for fabric on some scrap linen cloth. Sadly, however, the prints did not turn out well enough to be used on their own, as one was indistinct, the other slightly smudged, as you can see in the picture on the next page. My options with prints like these would have been relatively small; now, though, I can use Lutradur to camouflage the problem areas, whilst enhancing the strong parts of the prints, as well as giving extra colour and textural interest.

So, I decided to use them with some Lutradur that I had lying around. The prints, as you can see from the photographs, were brown on a white background, so I chose to use red and yellow colours to make it warmer. I tried some plain Lutradur, and whilst that did add texture, it did not add much in the way of visual interest. In the end, two particular pieces stood out as being suitable, so I prepared the postcards for quilting.

I took a piece of pelmet Vilene, cut to size, and some fusible mending tape. This comes in a narrow strip on a roll, and is ideal for using to fuse small pieces of fabric together. I cut strips to fit lengthwise, and fused the print to the Vilene. I then cut strips of the mending tape to fit across the top and bottom of the card, and fused the Lutradur onto the print. This method, though unusual, holds the layers still enough for machine quilting on a piece of this size; if you feel uncomfortable with it, though, you can add extra strips of mending tape to the cloth, or fuse the whole thing together with a piece of fusible web cut to size.

At this stage, though, you do need to consider if, or how, you will stitch the piece. If you wish to stitch by hand around the edges, for instance, make sure you place the fusible web a little way in from the edges themselves. This will make it much easier to stitch.

I then quilted the two pieces, seen above, ready to quilt. I try to use stitch in these small pieces to emphasise the relationship between the marks on the Lutradur and the marks on the underlying cloth. One of the pieces, when I looked at it, seemed to have more focus on the Lutradur patterning than on the print, so I quilted following the marks on the Lutradur. I did the reverse on the second card, quilting to emphasise the print rather than the colour and marks on the Lutradur. I then trimmed them both to finish them off, leaving the edges unfinished, as I intend to mount and frame them. Of course, Lutradur does not fray; if I had used felt (for example) between the Lutradur and the pelmet Vilene, rather than linen, I could have simply added a line of decorative or plain stitch at the edge of the piece. . This is an ideal way of trying out new stitches, new ideas for larger pieces etc. And if I wanted to send them through the mail as postcards, I would have zig zagged the edges, having first added a piece of plain white cloth to the back.

The finished pieces are shown below. Jungle Patterns, the piece on the left, was the piece quilted to emphasise the marks on the Lutradur, whilst 'Facing', was quilted to emphasise the underlying print. It is interesting to see how two very similar looking prints can turn out so differently, using the same techniques, but with a different emphasis each time. This is a great way of creating a series of work, where you can explore a particular design, using different colours, types of stitch, quilting patterns etc.

The finished postcards, 'Facing', left, and 'Jungle Patterns', right.

A detail of 'Facing', showing how the Lutradur interacts with the print below.

Project Five : Lutradur Through The Printer.

I enjoy printing photographs and other images on Lutradur, using the computer. As we've said before, the lighter weights are not ideal for using with a computer printer, though they can be ironed to freezer paper and fed carefully through. The heavier weights, though, are excellent for this purpose, can be cut to size and are firm enough to feed through the printer on their own. That said, the lighter weights can be run through a computer printer by backing them with freezer paper, but the images you get with the lighter weights are often indistinct, with much of the colour going straight onto the backing. However, you could use that partial image as a base layer, and add additional colour with transfer dyes. This can lead to interesting effects, particularly with abstract images.

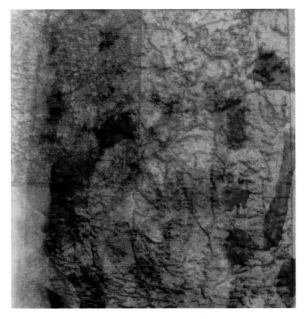

The image on the right shows a piece of computer printed Lutradur which has then had colour and further marks added to it, making a rather faded black and white piece into a colourful, interesting piece with potential. In fact, I had printed an image at the wrong size first time round, you can see it in the upper left hand side of the image. I corrected the size, and fed the same piece of Lutradur through the printer again, producing a rather unbalanced image. I then added colour in two layers; the first was a random piece of blue/green/red, the second consisted of a series of red marks. I wanted to try to draw attention away from the stronger printed area in the upper corner. The marks do that to a certain extent, and they echo the horizontal feeling that that area gives.

 Now, I will stitch into it, see what happens at that point, and possibly add more marks later. The piece has a working title of 'Dreamscape'; the colours and textures somehow seem to suggest dreams to me. I might add some text on paper, using collage, some poetry perhaps. It is always useful to take some time to consider how a piece might develop, even if that means storing it for months, or even years; when you come back to it, you will see it with a fresh eye. The more impatient among us, me included, can usually limit that to a week or so in a drawer.

Poster Party

Anyone who reads my blog knows that I have four cats, so it seemed reasonable that I would start making cat quilts, or 'Quilt Pets' as the series is known. I have some comedy cat fabric, with images of cats that look sinister, or odd in some way, and I wanted to use them in a quilt that would look like an old fashioned Wild West Wanted poster, as a fun addition to the series. I already had a small quilt made up, with one of the cats in the centre, so I started by printing individual words onto Lutradur.

To do that, I opened a new document in Microsoft Word, using Copperplate Gothic Bold typeface, as you can see in figure one. I then put the printer quality settings to 'best'; to do this, just follow the instructions in your printer manual. After printing, I cut out the words I wanted to use, and fused them onto the existing quilt. That worked reasonably well, as you can see from the picture below, but it was definitely lacking something. And despite a bit of judicious distressing with a heat gun, it still just didn't have the look I wanted. It just seemed too well preserved, somehow. And there was too much contrast between the Lutradur and the cloth beneath it.

I decided to develop the idea further by making a 'poster' entirely from Lutradur. The first artists to become interested in Lutradur were banner makers; the idea of a poster is drawn from that concept. I began by designing the poster itself, leaving enough room for an image, and printed it out. I then decided to 'age' it a little, by adding some colour, in this case watercolour from Lumin Arte, and when it was dry, fused on the image of my villain, the cat. And there he is, glaring out of the image, left.

As you can see, the Lutradur got a bit creased coming through the printer. I used that to my advantage in colouring the piece, as colour tends to collect in the creased parts of the Lutradur. In fact, a legitimate method of distressing Lutradur is simply to crumple it in your hand before stitching and colouring, as the colour will attach itself to the creases more so than to the flat surfaces.

That done, I wanted to age the piece a little, so I took a heat gun and carefully distressed the Lutradur, being careful not to overheat the Lutradur, so that it didn't melt entirely. I also used a soldering iron round the edges, to give an aged appearance, as well as making discrete holes in places, moving the soldering iron around to produce a variety of different shapes. You can see the results of using the soldering iron around the edges in the image on the right.

Remember, when heating Lutradur in order to distress it, you must work in a well ventilated area. Please refer to our health and safety instructions, if you have not already read them, before carrying out such processes.

WANTED

HAVE YOU SEEN THIS CAT?

RAY MOUSECHASER
CLAWED AND DANGEROUS
DO NOT APPROACH!

The finished piece

The final result is shown above; I photographed it on a dark background, so that you can see the variety of marks made by the different tools. The large holes were made with the soldering iron; the smaller, more diffused patterns of holes, with a heat gun. And as a final touch, I sprayed the completed piece with Print Guard, which is a UV water resistant varnish intended for ink jet and water soluble images (optional). I use this when I have been using water soluble images, including ink jet inks, as it gives a level of protection to the finished piece. Art pieces aren't usually washed, but accidents do happen!

The final example I wish to show you in this section is the way in which I used a photograph taken on a very wet day, through the windscreen of my car, whilst waiting in the car for a museum to open. I'm always far too early for everything, so make sure I have camera and journal with me always, as I hate wasting time. I thought that the smudgy feel of the piece might transfer well to Lutradur, given the inherent texture of the cloth. The original photograph is shown on the left, and shows halls of residence at the University of East Anglia in Norwich.

I began by manipulating the image. As this is not a book on computer use, I will not go into the processes I used in any great depth. Using Paint Shop Pro, I began by simply altering the contrast, resulting in the image below left, and then a second version, where I adjusted the hue and saturation of the image, producing a purple based version (right), which also pleased me.

I began to work with the images, selecting the blue/black one to focus on as being closest to the original in look and mood; the image above shows the piece as it came out on Lutradur, but on the reverse, rather than the front, to show the interesting texture that using the piece that way might have provided, as the fibres on the bottom of the transfer have not been affected by the dyes, leaving a whitish tinge over it. I decided not to use that side on this occasion, however, preferring the stronger contrast provided by the right side of the Lutradur.

I started by trimming the image. There was a diagonal line at the bottom, which was, in fact, the curve of the bottom of the car windscreen against the dashboard. I felt this was a distraction, and therefore removed it, and went on to trim both sides until I felt that the size was right.

I then had to think about how to add further colour. The computed printed lines that indicate the branches of the trees are quite fine, and some of them also quite pale, and I did not want the focal point of the image to disappear under a heavy layer of additional colour. And I wanted some variety in the colour, but for it also to remain as monochromatic as possible.

I had a piece of paper that had been used to monoprint an earlier piece which had got too much paint on it. It reminded me of the shape of the tree, and was not too dense. I decided to use a mask between the transfer dye and the cloth, in this case, a piece of Lutradur 30, which is ideal as a mask or filter in cases where you wish to add a lighter layer of textured colour than would usually be possible when using a strongly coloured background paper. The picture below shows a detail of the green grey dyed 'foliage' against the computer printed 'tree'. I was, however, concerned that the white of the uncoloured Lutradur was too consistent, so I fused a layer of light weight grey Vilene onto the back. This made the white appear to be mottled.

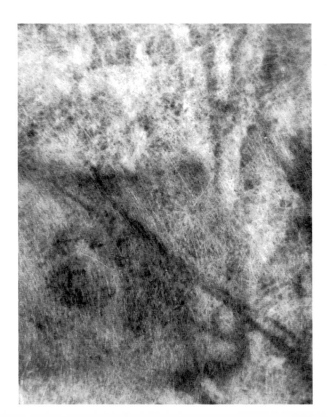

I then chose to mount it on a piece of black fabric; though it is not obvious from the photograph, the cloth has a rib effect (it is, in fact, the reverse of a vinyl treated cloth), and that itself adds more texture. And that, I thought, was that…until I noticed a piece of fine black netting on the floor. I wondered what the effect would be if I added it, so I ironed it and positioned it onto the piece (below right).

Though this development had potential, I decided to leave the first image as it is, and to experiment some more with the netting later. Finally, I had an image reminiscent of a photograph, but with interesting texture. I felt that stitch would overwhelm the delicate nature of the image, so decided to leave it as it was, though I did consider a single layer of machine stitch around the image, and may still do that. Sometimes, less really is more, and no matter how much we love to stitch, we have to work with the demands of each piece as it presents itself.

And that is where I left it, for the moment, anyway. As you can see, this initial exploration has the makings of a series of work. You have already seen two different options in this chapter; varying the colour of the printed image, and adding different materials. The possibilities are endless. And of course, there is an added advantage to using Lutradur as a mask. You do end up with a lovely extra piece of cloth (see below), which can be used in another project. I did consider that yet another option would be to use this Lutradur over one of the coloured versions of this image, to see what it would be like. Why not try it, and see?

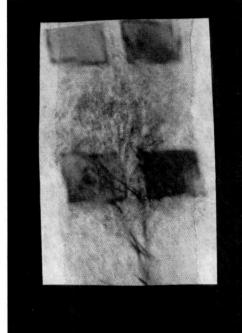

Project Six : Altered Quilts

I enjoy altering things; I make altered books, and have been known to alter other things, such as shoes, boxes and the like. So, I thought, why can't I alter a quilt? Sometimes, no matter what you do to a particular piece, it just doesn't come out right. I have a particular interest in pieces like that, and have been known to 'rescue' other peoples' work when they get to the point when they can't think of anything else to do, but equally don't want to throw the piece out. I'm sure we can all identify with that particular feeling.

Lutradur is a highly flexible material, and can be used over ostensibly finished pieces very easily. The piece I will talk about here is a small piece that I was not at all happy with (pictured right). I had made a lino print using black printing ink on some very soft beige handmade paper, and stitched into it, only to discover that the finished article looked very flat. So I painted into the design, and added some acrylic metallic medium, in an attempt to give the surrounding areas more depth and visual interest. That was an improvement, but it somehow lacked that spark that makes a good piece. So it lay around my sewing studio for about six months, being moved from place to place, while I tried to think what to do.

I finally decided to do something about it (basically, I got tired of moving it around!). As in the earlier project with the postcards, I tried out various possibilities, as you will see in the image below. I did have several clear ideas in mind when auditioning these fabrics. Firstly, I wanted to pick up the yellow colour that had been painted into the lino print, and which had also been used to stitch in certain areas of the quilt. I also wanted to find a piece that would add some visual texture to the really flat areas surrounding

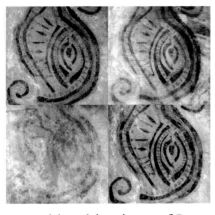

the print itself, as these seemed boring in comparison with the rest of the piece.

Working clockwise from the first image in this collage, the first piece of Lutradur I tried was too close to the colour of the original piece. The result was that the quilt still looked just as bland as it did without the Lutradur, as there was very little variation in either colour or tone. In fact, even the yellow seems to be muted by this piece of Lutradur.

The second piece was, in some ways, just as bad. The yellow in it overwhelmed the yellow in the painting, as it turned all the rest of the painting into a yellow morass. And in addition, the marks at the right hand side of this piece of Lutradur are distracting. They are too bright against the rest of the piece, and introduce a sideways movement that detracts from the strength of the main motif.

The third piece of Lutradur might have been good, as it had much more visual interest. However, as this is a heavier weight of Lutradur (100gm as opposed to 30gm), the transparency is much diminished, and the yellow motifs have disappeared entirely. This was not the result I was aiming for. However, this piece does have potential for a different result. Had I been prepared to concentrate on the linoprint alone, I might have added this particular piece of Lutradur, stitched around the edges of the black printed marks, and then cut away the Lutradur, as Dijanne did in the first project. I did consider this as a possibility, but rejected it; I will, however, look to use this piece of Lutradur in that way with another print.

The fourth piece of Lutradur, however, whilst not being perfect, does have a variety of colour, which encourages the eye to travel round the piece. It adds some visual texture to the sides, and the yellow areas do show through quite well. So I decided to go with that.

I cut the piece to size, trying it both ways before deciding which orientation to choose. It is worth remembering at this stage that Lutradur has no grain, and does not fray. It is possible to fussy cut it, if the piece is large enough, so that the most interesting parts of the cloth are featured on the finished work. If you have to cut it diagonally to do so, it's not a problem!

For this project, I wanted to show you how easy it is to use scrap pieces of Lutradur in order to alter an existing piece of work. However, if I had not had anything suitable in my stash, I would have custom made a piece for this project. Fortunately, though, a suitable piece was to hand, as the quilt itself is a small one. And below, the finished quilt.

Designing The Quilting.

The piece had already been quite extensively quilted, so I didn't want to add too much stitch, as the existing stitch is clearly visible below the Lutradur. Since I wanted to focus on the yellow in the underlying piece, I decided to cut away the Lutradur in the areas where yellow featured, in this case, within the main part of the print, and within the spirals at either side. It is really important, when altering a quilt like this, to integrate the Lutradur with the piece below. Both the print itself and the stitching show through the Lutradur, and there needs to be some connection between both layers to make a cohesive piece. Therefore, I stitched round those areas using a fuchsia coloured thread, which, as well as showing up on the black printed areas and contrasting with the yellow, brings up the colour of the red spots throughout the piece. To strengthen the cohesion, I then added a little more stitching; more fuchsia in the centre of the image, in a circle, to echo the circles I had already stitched in the hearts of each spiral. I then edged the red painted circles at the bottom of the piece with fuchsia also, to give extra visual interest and reinforce the idea of the circular images.

Finishing The Edges

I hate binding. Most of my work does not have finished edges, and that is a deliberate choice, but sometimes a piece requires a more streamlined look. This is the technique I used on this particular piece.

I decided to finish off the piece using the technique I usually use on larger quilts. You do need to do a bit of thinking beforehand; the Lutradur on top must be larger than the finished top by around half an inch, and the quilting must stop before the edges of the piece all the way round. In this case, there is stitching right to the edge of the original quilt, but of course, that is beneath the Lutradur; the stitching on top is limited to a few strategic lines and shapes, as we discussed earlier.

Lie the piece face down on the ironing board, and insert a piece of mending tape between the Lutradur and the rest of the piece. Using the tip of your iron, press down through the quilt in several places, to 'tack' down the mending tape (optional in a small piece, which should be easy to handle). In the image below, you can see what happens next; the Lutradur and the mending tape are brought over the edge of the quilt and fused. Continue in this way around the quilt, making your corners square or mitred as you wish. As Lutradur does not fray, no further stitching is required. This is a quick and effective way of finishing small pieces. 'Building Blocks' (see gallery) is finished in that way.

In the image, here, you can see how the mending tape tucks in neatly between the Lutradur and the finished surface. This can also be used to finish off 'unaltered' or original quilts, of course! You may choose to stitch around the edges for definition or other decorative purposes, but it is not necessary to do so.

Section Three: Gallery

A lot can be learned from simply looking at other peoples' work. Of course, it's best to do this 'in the flesh', by visiting shows, exhibits and galleries, but a set of photographs is the next best thing. Here, we have combined a series of images of work we have created recently, to try to show you how versatile Lutradur can be. We also wanted to highlight just how differently we work with the same material; Lutradur provides enormous scope for textile practitioners to experiment and discover new techniques and ideas.

Marion : Alien Landscapes 2006, Lutradur on cotton. This small quilt has a rich coloured surface. Using some of the marks I had made as a starting place, I began to draw with thread, and a landscape emerged.

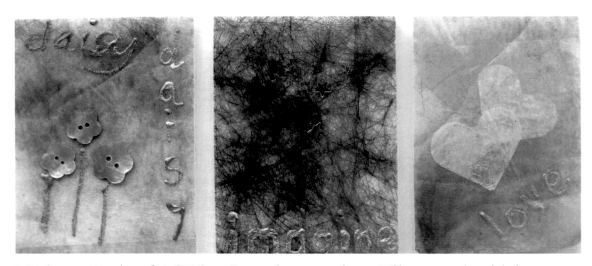

Marion : A trio of ACEOs. Lutradur on pelmet Vilene, each with its own embellishments. I didn't feel there was a need to add stitch at all to these; there was enough visual interest in the lutradur itself, and the embellishments.

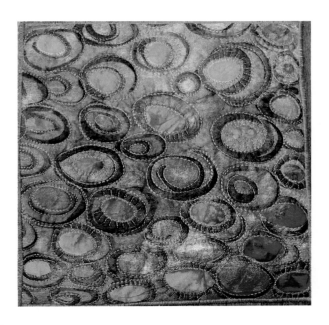

Dijanne: Blue Spots. On this piece, I painted the blue swirls on the paper and transferred it to coloured lutradur. I then stitched around the circle shapes in contrasting thread to highlight the circles, and in some areas, cut away the lutradur to reveal the rich blue colour underneath.

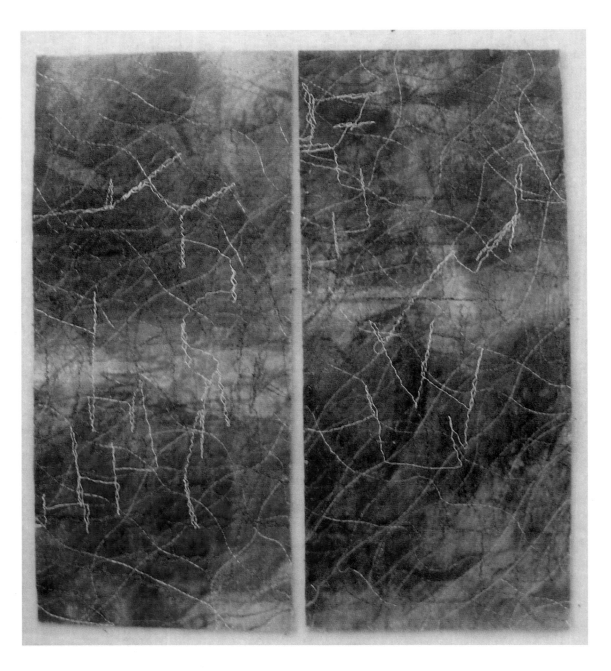

Marion : Storm Diptych 2007. Lutradur on hand printed cotton and velvet.
Intensive stitch is layered over these pieces in several different colours,
creating a tension of sorts. I almost expect to hear the rumble of thunder in
the distance.

Dijanne: Moody River After the Storm. The colours suggests a river calming down after a storm, perhaps after Marion's Storm pieces- the river slowly finding equilibrium again. The river itself has been foiled and cut away and accentuated with heavy machine stitching balanced by some hand stitching.

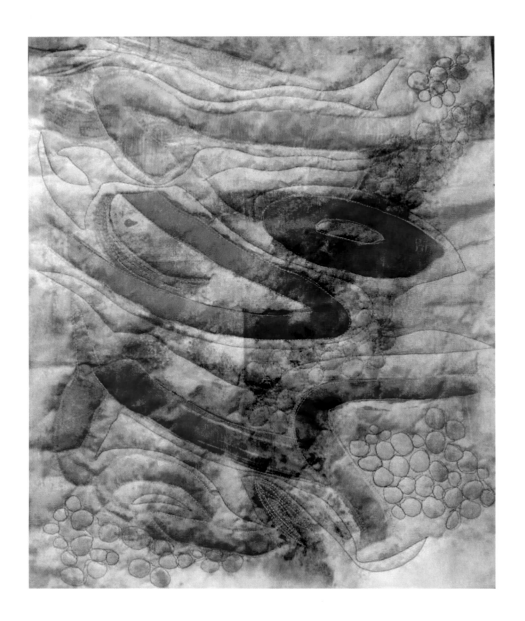

Marion : Alternative Landscapes, 2008. Lutradur over hand printed cotton.
Landscapes seem to be turning up in my work quite regularly now, whether
I like it or not! This piece began as a deconstructed screenprint printed out
over large scale bubble wrap, producing the small circles that are a feature
of the piece.

Marion : Star Swirl, 2005. Lutradur over velvet with appliquéd cotton and embellishments. Note the dense stitch bringing out the density of the velvet below the lutradur.

Marion : Connections, 2008. Lutradur with embellished fibres. Another example of drawing with stitch; this time, I also added fibres, using the embellisher machine. Lutradur is an ideal base fabric for embellishment.

Marion : Temple of the Sun God. Lutradur over painted cotton, foiled.
This piece, made from 100gm lutradur, was printed using several different
designs to add texture and interest. I struggled to decide which way up it
was meant to be, before deciding that this was the right way up!

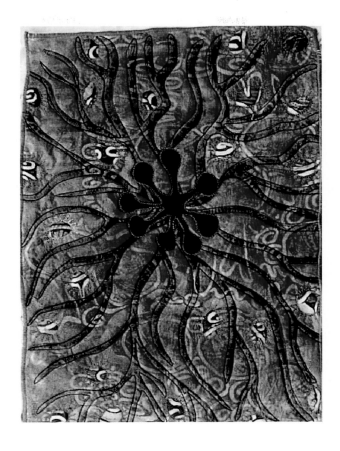

Dijanne: The central motif has been inspired by an Adinkra stamp placed over a nebulous tree shape- suggesting connections. The underlying fabric has been hand painted and areas snipped away to suggest precious patterns. This particular adinkra symbol is FOFO "yellow flowered plant", symbol of jealousy and envy. "When the fofo's petals drop, they turn into black spiky-like seeds. The Akan liken the nature of this plant to a jealous person."

- The Adinkra Dictionary by W. Bruce Willis. More information can be found here:
<http://www.welltempered.net/adinkra/htmls/adinkra/fofo.htm>

Marion : Red Dot, 2006. Lutradur over commercial red velvet, with appliquéd cotton. Because lutradur does not fray, it is ideal for pieces with uneven edges.

Dijanne- Red poppies. I created a lino-cut of the poppy format and printed that onto pre-coloured lutradur then cut away the petals. I think this might have worked better if there had been greater contrast in the background fabric.

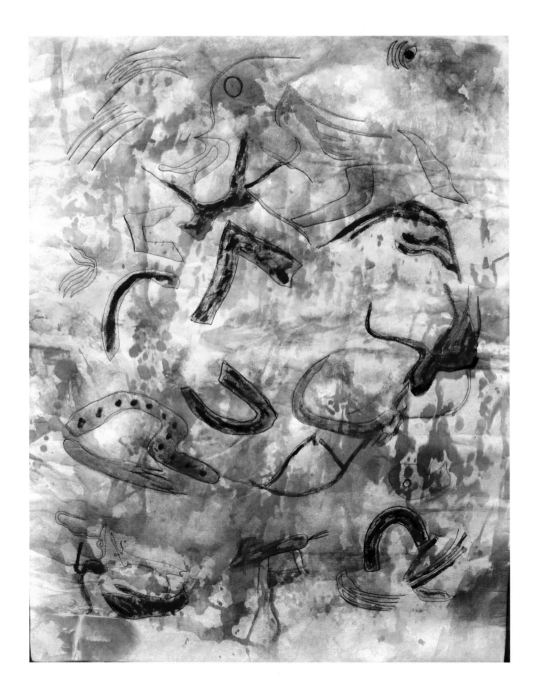

Marion : Underlying Causes, 2006. Lutradur on painted cloth. There were some interesting marks below the lutradur, suggesting cave paintings, but stitch alone was not enough to make them distinctive. I therefore added acrylic paint to the stitched marks, and continued to draw with the thread (as in the eye in the top right hand corner). The same technique was used with Forgotten Flights (2006), below.

Marion : Forgotten Flights, 2007. 100gm lutradur. This particular type of lutradur is as good used on its own as a cloth, as it is used in combination with other patterned cloths below to make a combined image. The edging is a rayon yarn which is an exact match to the acrylic paint used to show the details.

Marion : Monolith, 2006. Lutradur on hand painted and pieced cotton. An 'altered quilt'. The sections of the pieced quilt below the lutradur were at war with each other; a layer of lutradur unified the piece. Note the yellow stitching uniting the yellow areas of the quilt and continuing through the rest of the piece. Many of the marks were added after the lutradur was stitched onto the cloth; it took quite a while to get the balance absolutely right.

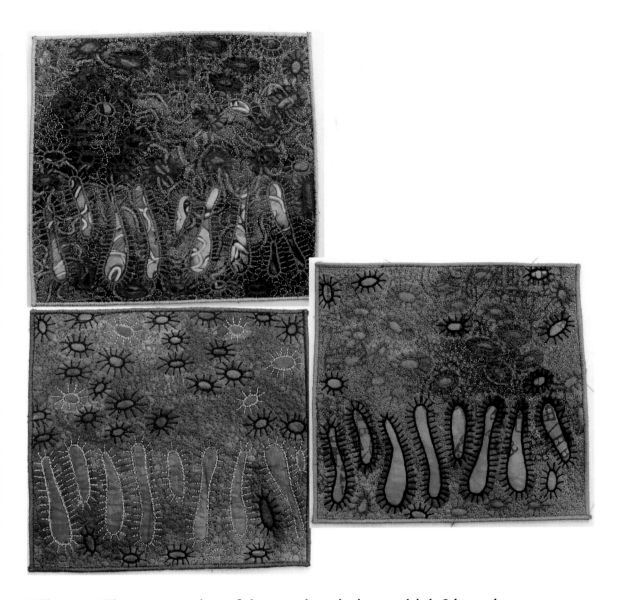

Dijanne: Three examples of the coral variations which I have been working on for the last year. I like experimenting with the interplay of fabric colour and line colour

Marion : American Dreams 2008. Lutradur. This is another altered quilt; it was originally an unsuccessful lutradur quilt. I cut it up into several pieces, and used fabric crayons and acrylic paint to add colour contrast and visual interest to the piece. I added much of the colour by following the stitch lines, which made the piece coherent as well as more colourful.

Peaks And Troughs Detail (see next page).

Marion : Peaks And Troughs, 2006. Lutradur on hand dyed cotton. This piece features cut away lutradur in several places, including the spiral in the top centre of the quilt, shown in the detail here. The painted lines are of acrylic paint on a transfer dyed cloth; the layer below is a vintage cotton tablecloth which was hand dyed.

Dijanne: "X" Marks the Place- in the past three years I have done a lot of travelling in the Middle East and have become fascinated by the cross stitching used on much of the clothing and utilitarian items. Patterns speak of heritage and identity. Interestingly, an "X" is also used to denote agreement by people who are illiterate. Something so simple, yet loaded with meaning and ownership. These pieces have been created painting the crosses onto papers and then transferring them and I have used free form cross stitch to enhance the effect. This is a series of three pieces worked in different colours to highlight individuality and personality in even something as simple as an "X"

Marion : Texture Of Memory VI, Torn. Lutradur, pelmet Vilene. This is made from two layers of distressed lutradur over pelmet Vilene, embellished with fibres and a glass cabochon made by Mickey and Madeline Art Glass, trading on Etsy as Gimmebeads. The text was written directly onto the pelmet Vilene, and can still be read through the lutradur layers.

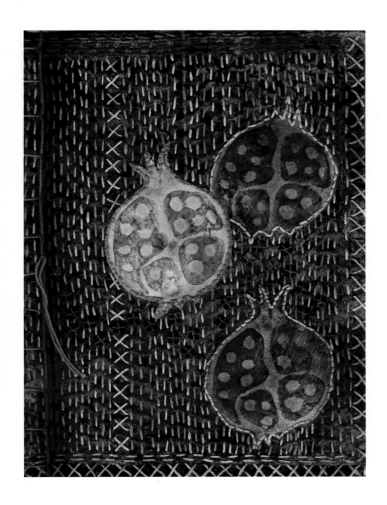

Dijanne: Pomegranates are a favourite symbol- not only suggesting connection with the Greek classic tale of Demeter and her search for her daughter Persephone but in recent times a more poignant reminder of connections with my own daughters. In the Middle East, the fruit of the pomegranate is revered for its health giving qualities. There is something enticing about the rich lush fruit. This is actually a book cover for a book about Pomegranates; the back cover is shown below right.

Marion : Lost Planet, 2008. Lutradur on monoprinted cotton. Another piece featuring Mike's wonderful art glass, one of six small pieces I commissioned to use with art textiles. The circles are made by drawing with gutta, as well as with stitch, and reflect the circular marks on the linen below the lutradur, which were made by monoprinting.

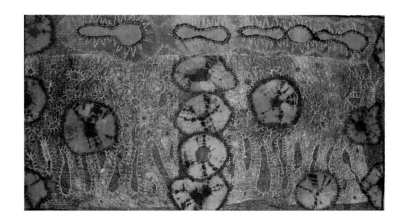

Dijanne: Another book cover- employing the coral linocut. The linocut has been printed onto the lutradur and then sewn onto momogami paper. Momogami papers are Japanese and were once used by the poor to make clothing because of its quality of strength. The piece has then been overlaid with tie dyed circles.

Dijanne: Box Gum (detail, below right, full piece, next page).
 I often create work with rivers- rivers are the lifeblood of Australia. We are an incredibly dry continent and without rivers we could very well be all desert. The river panel in the centre of the quilt has been created with lutradur and foiling. This quilt also illustrates my passion for hand dyed cloth using simple resist techniques. The box gum is a favourite gum tree- the roundness of the leaf is somehow very appealing.

Section Four : Troubleshooting

Nothing ever works the way you expect it to! Nine times out of ten, things will go beautifully, but that tenth time, things will go wrong. In this section, we have tried to identify the kinds of things you might need to know in order to save the day.

I'm having difficulty mixing the dye into a smooth paste.

Try using a bit more hot water, and an electric hand whisk. Works every time, and it is Marion's preferred mode of mixing for larger amounts. Please do keep a dedicated hand whisk for this purpose; food preparation and dye powder don't mix. No pun intended.

I can't get colour to transfer from the paper to the cloth.

There could be several reasons for that.

1. Your iron does not heat up enough to transfer the colour; try another iron.
2. Your iron is not on the correct setting; make sure it is at maximum.
3. You haven't waited long enough for the iron to heat up (those of us who are keen, do this…). Give it ten minutes, have a cup of coffee and try again.
4. The humidity in the air is low. If you have a steam iron, float it above the paper over the Lutradur, and put out a jet of steam. Do NOT let the iron touch the paper, and do keep your hand well out of the way. Switch the steam back off and iron in the usual way.
5. There might not have been enough dye powder in your initial mix, if you mixed it from powder. Add more dye to your mix and try again.
6. The paper you may be using might be creating the problem. The surface of the paper and its absorption rate can play a role.
7. Check that the paper is painted side down, as both sides can look very similar – the right side usually has more detail.

The paper has stuck to the cloth

Ouch! Get as much of the rest of the paper off the cloth as you can, leaving only the pieces that are stuck. Let it cool, then spray gently with cold water, let it soak in a bit and then gently try to peel it off. Sometimes it works, sometimes it doesn't. That said, the paper can add an interesting texture.

Incidentally, if you are adding more colour to cloth after other processes, remember that anything glue based already on the cloth *will* stick it to the paper, and no amount of damping, teasing and peeling will get it to come off. Yes, this has happened to Marion.

I'm not happy with the results from transfer dyeing.

Depends what you aren't happy about. Once the dye is transferred to the cloth, it is there for good. However, you do have a number of options. You could;

1. Overdye with more of the same colour
2. Overdye with a contrasting colour
3. Overdye with a printed paper
4. Overdye using a stencil, as in the foiling project, but adding transfer dye instead of glue
5. Tear up pieces of dyed paper, add them to your piece at random and then iron it on.
6. Add more colour using acrylics etc
7. Fuse it onto another, contrasting piece of Lutradur. Add a lightweight piece if your original piece is, say, Lutradur 100, and vice versa.
8. You could try stitching into it at this point, particularly if it is a heavier weight of cloth. The results can be surprising, and if you feel there is a need for still more colour, you can add it after stitching. Using a heavy weight thread and hand stitching can do amazing things, particularly if you use rayon threads.

I've burnt a hole in the Lutradur.

Sorry, there's nothing we can do about that one. Other than suggest you hang onto it, as it might come in useful in a piece where you are using distressed fabrics. On the other hands holes can be interesting in their own right! You will be able to duplicate the colours on another piece of Lutradur, as you can get up to three prints from one piece of painted paper, so all is not lost. And fortunately, with Lutradur, it doesn't happen all that often. To avoid doing this, keep the iron moving all the time.

With the thinner cloths (see the introduction), you could try lowering the temperature of the iron slightly; it then becomes a balancing act between the temperature needed for colour transfer, and that needed to keep the cloth in one piece. Not easy; if you are not sure about a particular piece of cloth, test it first.

Is there any type of paint I should avoid with Lutradur?

We wouldn't recommend oil paints at this point. Other than that, anything in your armoury is likely to be useable with Lutradur; make test pieces and record the results in a journal.

Can I add transfer dyes over, say, acrylic paint?

Yes, you can. Transfer dyes seem to show up quite well over all the different surfaces we've tested, making it a good way of adding extra detail to an almost finished piece.

My Lutradur got stuck in the printer.

Another ouch. To avoid this,

1. make sure you trim the Lutradur to the correct size
2. make sure that it is completely flat, no creases, especially at the top
3. try feeding it in by hand

I'm not happy with the images that I've printed out from the computer.

1. Check the settings of your printer. I print my Lutradur using the 'best' option on my HP printer.
2. Make sure that the image you are using has a lot of contrast. If there are a lot of pale colours in the image, they won't show up well against the Lutradur. This is especially true if there is a lot of detail in the images, some of which will be lost.

Section Five : Appendices

Appendix 1 : Suppliers List

A selection of suppliers, who stock dyes, Lutradur or both. Inclusion in this list is not a recommendation, nor is this an exhaustive list.

Europe:

Galerie Smend; http://www.smend.de/shop/index.html

Dreamline: http://www.dreamline.nl/

Zijdelings: http://www.zijdelings.com/

Trapsuutjies;http://www.trapsuutjies.nl/

Quilt und Textilkunst Muenchen: www.quiltundtextilkunst.de

Australia:

KraftKolour: http://www.kraftkolour.com.au/

The Thread Studio; http://www.thethreadstudio.com/

Zartworks; http://www.zartart.com.au/html/zartworkscontact.html

Batik Oetoro : http://www.dyeman.com

New Zealand:

Tillia Dyes; http://www.tillia.co.nz/

United Kingdom:

ArtVanGo; http://www.artvango.co.uk/

ColourCraft Ltd; http://www.colourcraftltd.com/

Kemtex; http://www.kemtex.co.uk/kemtexreact.htm

Rainbow Silks; http://www/rainbowsilks.co.uk

Spunart : http://www.spunart.co.uk

USA:

Joggles; http://www.joggles.com

MisterArt; http://www.misterart.com

PRO Chemical & Dye: http://www.prochemical.com

Appendix 2 : Artists Profiles

Marion Barnett

Marion is a Scottish artist living and working in a
tiny village in Norfolk, UK with four cats, lots of art
supplies, sundry musical instruments, including a lute, and a very
understanding spouse. She was introduced to Lutradur by Dijanne, several
years ago, immediately fell in love with it, and has made it the focus of her
textile work ever since. She also uses it in her mixed media and altered art
work, and intends to extend that to using Lutradur as a base for paintings.

Her work has always featured texture and colour; learning to paint has also
introduced an interest in line, particularly drawing with stitch.

Marion's work has been exhibited in the UK, Europe and the USA. She
has demonstrated and taught at quilt shows, including the Scottish Quilt
Championships and ExpoMagicQuilt in Lyon, and is available to give talks
and workshops and individual coaching; email for more details
(artmixter@tiscali.co.uk). She is currently writing her first solo book,
'Finding Your Creative Focus', a book about beating creative blocks, as
well as Exquisite Evolon, about another non-woven polyester cloth. An
avid blogger, her work can be found online in several places, including;

http://artmixter.blogspot.com

http://artmixter.etsy.com

http://www.thegallerydereham.co.uk

http://www.thedb.com/artmixter